CONTROLLED BURN

Controlled Burn

Maury Wrubleski

THISTLEDOWN PRESS

Canadian Cataloguing in Publication Data

Wrubleski, Maury, 1960–
Controlled burn
(New leaf editions. Series six)
Poems.
ISBN 1-895449-99-5
I. Title. II. Series.
PS8595.R96C65 1999   C811'.54   C99-920196-4
PR9199.3.W793C65 1999

Cover illustration by J. Forrie
Typeset by Thistledown Press Ltd.
Printed and bound in Canada

Thistledown Press Ltd.
633 Main Street
Saskatoon, Saskatchewan
S7H 0J8

ACKNOWLEDGEMENTS

The author would like to thank Tim Lilburn, Don McKay, Dennis Cooley, and Rod MacIntyre for their generous help and encouragement. Thanks to Ruth Smillie and the Globe Theatre for their work on the production of "Del T. and the Age of Jazz" at the On Line Cabaret. Special thanks to the students, staff, and the Board of Education of the Humboldt Collegiate Institute for their continuing support.
Poems from this manuscript have previously appeared in *Grain*, *NeWest Review*, *The Fiddlehead*, and the *Antigonish Review*.

Canadian   Patrimoine
Heritage   canadien

Thistledown Press gratefully acknowledges the financial assistance of the Canada Council for the Arts, the Saskatchewan Arts Board, and the Government of Canada through the Book Publishing Industry Development Program for its publishing program.

CONTROLLED BURN

CONTENTS

HEALING GROUND

BORDERS

for my family

HORSE SENSE

before the foal's birth   this abundant distance
          this transcendental darkness folds
                                        against itself   repleats
          wears a seam   thin
                    friction thin   separates
flicks a faint   hoof
          resolves to figures

colours penetrate
          leopard paint roan buckskin chestnut
                    lightless colours illuminated by odours
long musical legs
                    polychromatic   muscle and hide
hair hued curling in smoke
                    long maned rivulets diffusing darkness
                                        refusing into dapples
                    steam rising with crap heap combustion incense
lightless
                    not colours in a conventional sense
                                        visual cross referencing that
demands a diction of its own
          Equus Icarus
          life drawn to light —
                                        then creature contact

There is wetness on my chest, hot cold steam,
an amniotic bath. My eyes widen, the knowledge of genitalia.
Legs spindle tender tendon mesh jointed
shoulders ball and cock, connect with air and finally the ground.
Muscle bone marrow, flesh from flesh
crowning into mortality;
I no longer know where wet ends and flesh begins.
This huge wet thing, more characteristics than whole
pulses with newness
steams alive, caramel coated
stained in colours that wait for the invention of words.
Slurp,

9

salutatory and salivatory-
wetness on my hand,
a meeting,
a way of opening ourselves,
a winking to acknowledge the duplicity of this dual bondage.
You shit, I shovel
I hook, you haul
I cool you, rub down the race day sweat;
you cool, restore your breathing to domestic.
I rub off the primeval,
the plains.
In the foam is the haunt of wilderness.

The day we tumble the rail fence,
victims of a title defense in a stock saddle race,
I bounce — meal sack — to the ground but
you charge the heroic path through, splitting the rail
which bores into ground on one end and
propels up on the other, into your chest. You stumble, speared.
The field thunders into the first corner,
traffic flowing past a single roll over.
Again, wetness on my arm, capillaries and nerves pull together
wave and spark.
I am embarrassed by the sudden whiteness of my bone
in contrast to the spruce rail yellow of yours,
worn in your soft flesh,
yellow and dappled crimson to my pallor,
crimson
            which
the air refuses but the ground receives.
I look at you
you stare back, blameless,
through your wound.
You and I have opened to each other
in a new way.

The kid straightens himself out of the barn, shortening Tango's lead line. He feels the halter shank, end folded, not coiled, the tightness of his left fist. Feels the burn of the rope across his right hand, yet to come. The old man's eyes burn into the kid's neck. The kid winces; with every step the stallion's chest gathers like a storm, hindquarters spooled. Kid fights his own muscles, puffing away horseflies as he wraps the rope around a thick poplar. He hitches a sloppy knot, frets, grounds himself to retie it. Hooves skitter the grasshoppers as the kid steers back end toward the barn — watch the back leg, watch the back leg, and he breathes himself back into shape before receding into the waiting stall shit.

Back he goes when you're done. Right?

Outside, Tango worked at fury. Fury, not a natural state; a black science to be mastered. Genetic retroburst, a throwback organ from thousands of years, before horses dodged Cree and Blackfoot, from when they wintered low and summered high. Pumping systalic rage, ancestral blood, choler, venom, seminal dreams of manes flying, eyes bolt brilliant, breath crimson against hoodoos and curtains of dust, pushed by vane gales under a nimbus gathering. Layers of porch story romanticism. A calculated fury, allowing one's capture to pitch against a force. Ripe to the possibilities, courting the shank. Rage without resistance is nothing.

The old man does a delivery run every three weeks for the local market — cattle, horses, sheep. Two pickups to do. Sale day tomorrow.

No goddamn brains. None at all. I shoulda nutted that crazy bastard when I had the chance. McMillan's stud and Butterscotch as a dam . . . God . . . that made for a nice lookin' horse. He's muscled like nobody's business. Sixteen hands of him. Jesus, him and that chestnut, they'd throw nice colts. Or even put him up against one of those crazy Appaloosa mares of your sisters — if it throws a blanket, who knows. But what the hell good is he as he is?

Not a brain in his goddamn head. Stupid bastard's gonna snap that halter shank if he keeps jerkin' his head around like that. Don't leave'm tethered to that poplar. Better stick'm back in the barn before we go.

Twenty or twenty-five miles down the road, curses and tobacco spit run down the old man's shirt. Kid sits next to him in the cab of the three ton, juiced up to hang over the stock racks, electric prod in hand.

That's the thing about horses. It doesn't matter what kinda frame you get if they ain't got the brains to work with ya. Take Calypso — at four years old, he's workin' into the best damn cuttin' horse I've seen in years. Same dam, eh — but a different stud. Not quite as big as that crazy sorrel, but even tempered an' sharp as a whip . . .

First pickup. The kid bounces with know-how. Reads comics at the same time, eats head cheese sandwiches, gnaws with the rhythm of ruts.

Now I don't say you gotta knock sense into 'em. More often than not, that's gonna do more harm than good. But you can't be scared to be firm either. If a horse wants to do you in every time you get on him, well — you just gotta work him. Take the piss an' vinegar out've him. Put him on a lunge line. Work it out of him. He'll generly come 'round before you know it.

Second pickup. The old man's talking crop too long. Kid hangs his arm out the window, lets an old collie lick his hand. Clutches the cattle prod in the other hand.

To see him today you wouldn't believe it. Ol' Nick said you couldn't do nothing with that rang-a-tang buckskin of Marshalls but he worked him with a hackamore for a few weeks. I hate them things. I told 'im so too. I told him to use a snaffle bit instead, but Nick's got more luck than judgement

an' pretty soon, damned if that buckskin isn't comin' around.
That's all it takes — we get home, first thing in the mornin', we
dig Ol' numbnuts outta his boxstall and —

Shit.

Kid's eyes get wide. Breathing gets shallow with fear. The road home.
Fear of the stallion, fear to tell. Secret hammering like hooves.

The stallion runs upside down, caught in a drastic stillness, frame
frozen, a free range pony painting. No hoodoos and the dust has
settled. Fire form mane spreads aloft on the ground. Front fetlock
wrapped in a halter shank, leg extends, leaping over the line, leaping
its own tendons. Eyes all glass wired, wide. Neck stretched, pre-rigor
reach, suspended by violence. The tree bark has peeled like fruit rind.
Poplar veins split the sky.

The first dead thing the kid has ever seen.

CALYPSO

How would a kid get that this mountain of flesh bone
and mane was named
Calypso
    seventeen hands high, an island for a rump
    half-acre hooves with the white, Clydesdale feathers draped into
the dust, no hint of Trinidadian sprites
in your stoop, just your name
a two syllable echo of your gait when
the old man tosses the kid on your back
clip
        sho   clip
                         slow
two step
        grid road
clop shoe
        shuffle
        but
              slide
you could dance
                when the old man got on you
made you
        pivot
        on a
      hind leg change leads snap
      your hooves forward cut
in   lean around
     a pole your neck arched
        like an Arab with a dished-in doll face
show off
your hunch settles in the evening under a kid and a saddle with
shortened stirrups
the flamenco
    the limbo tucked
away into mane
        the folds
  of your name

Bruce is Tired in Yellow Grass

Bruce is tired in Yellow Grass.
Little need for a familial frame of reference
to offer proof.
It's in the eyes
supine glance beyond the sweetgrass horizon
eyes swimming in the sun, begging heat in winter
cool in summer.
In the roots
stretching into brown loam, craving transplant.
In the drowning
in a sea of wheat and family,
small town rhetoric and local board policy.

Captive in a mosaic of ghosts and prophets
and middle age.
Marching in twelve step increments towards
a geographical salvation.

He is not tied to a mortgage
but he is tied to the land.
A creeping cancerous precept that keeps him
chained, stable as equinox,
to this land of frozen sun.

His comfort was looking at the stars, but he has grown
weary with their constancy.
He searches the night sky only for man-made anomalies
for Russian satellites that reflect sunlight
into polar chambers.

He crosses himself with his future,
blesses the occasional diversion.
He repents for everything,
in retrospect,
he knows that he has done right.

PATRICK DANCES ON LITTLE MANITOU

When you left,
you chalked it up to the weight and spin of your life,
and not your father's death. The inertia that dictated your staying,
realized your leaving.
Wingless, groundless, margined, mainstream,
all of these at any given time.

You felt the leaving when you packed
that picture, the one of you and him on the ferry,
your only visit to the coast. You steered the boat,
sea curdled in long wakes, stroking where you had been.
Dream of those days with the weight of whales,
where he almost danced, a gangling step as he
swept down,
ladled you into his arms, hoisted you to that
wide-shouldered mizzenmast,
told you to call from your crow's nest if you spied any ports o' call.
You drummed an advance on the brim of his cap.

Salt shot roar at the epicenter of what shook him alive.
Sea-spray countered the drag of the prairie wind.
Of the father's lumberyard grind, days and days of night watching.

His blue on blue horizon, islands like floating kids.

You have settled, saline charmed, on the low slung
shore of this salt lake.
Consciously breathing, filtering sulfur and magnesium,
you kick your own salt spray, a trick of geography.
Dance on the shores of this lake, your father's clumsy pirouette,
legs boat walk rocking.
Dance with a woman your father never knew.

MAGPIES

The world stank of woodsmoke at 6 a.m. in the old man's house.
Even in the summer, the air was still damp enough to catch it and
pummel it down into an inversion haze over the hollow. Almost every
morning, before we kids got back from squatting against the cold lid in
the outhouse,
Anthony and Moses
would cross the last barbed wire gate into the yard from their camp
in the back pasture.
Every summer, sure as migration, Silverquill would show up on the
doorstep with the missus and Anthony and Moses and the rest of the
kids looking for a couple weeks work.
Whatever happened to be on hand at the time . . .
hauling in last year's bales . . .
breaking horses.
And after that they'd pack up back for the reserve or head north to
Nut Lake and do God knows what. They camped in the pasture in an
old tarp tent that we figured looked for all the world like a teepee.
Anthony and Moses
would come up on the first morning looking for us to play.
We invented games or we stuck with the traditional cowboys and
Indians where Anthony and I would be the cowboys and leave the
young kids, Moses and my nephew, to be the Indians. Most of those
games translated into Anthony and I taking off to the abandoned farm
house across the pasture leaving the little kids to stew and tattle for
the rest of the day.
One weekend, after a cheque came in,
Silverquill took his family down to Yorkton for the fair.
Without the boys to play with, my nephew and I took to proving
a theory that the old man put us on a few days before.
Magpies

       Magpies . . . they crawled all over everything
alive or dead and they sat in the trees and squawked and bitched
and played smug over everything.

The old man told us that if you killed one and hung it up in a tree, that the rest of them would take off. You wouldn't see a magpie for days. And aside from the attraction of killing one, the remedy seemed too easy and it begged to be proved.

So the old man armed us with a 410 shotgun
(I was the only one of us boys who was to use it so I relished the job all the more)
and sent us off away from the livestock to hunt one down and hang it from the poplar tree up by the pump. Sweet vengeance.
We'd missed so many with rocks that the magpies figured their chances pretty good that morning. But in half an hour, we popped off three and gingerly grabbed them by their scaly warm legs and strung them up
in the tree.
And to our amazement, not a magpie showed up
curious, bereaved, or otherwise. (At least not until the noise from the 410
and our whooping died down.)
And we kids waited for Anthony and Moses to show up again
to show them our trophies and enlist them for
the next hunt.
Two days later
Silverquill and the boys showed up
(without any money but with what seemed to be a half-trunk full of canned ham and a couple boxes of snuff for the old man).
Anthony and Moses came up from the camp and my nephew and I fought over who was going to show them the magpies.
It didn't matter.
You couldn't miss the carcasses twisting in the branches.
And they were starting to stink anyhow.
I know Anthony saw them there. What I couldn't figure out was why he grabbed Moses around the neck, twisted him around and set him running hell bent out of the yard. They almost trampled one another getting back to their camp. And neither of them came up to the yard for the rest of the day.

My nephew and I were left to ponder our offense.

That night, we went through the pasture to the camp. Nobody wanted to talk about the magpies. Silverquill opened a can of ham and boiled potatoes on the fire and we shared it with the family. We all talked about the Yorkton Fair and the Fishing Lake chuckwagon races. Nobody talked about the magpies.

The next morning, I went out, took down the remains and tossed them in the garbage pit before anybody else got up.

WANDERLUST

Time is a great teacher said my grandpa, himself
a teacher.
Life
a set-up to the great lesson.
Life
a journey.

Time, to a kid growing up, weedy
is a slow, mostly unwritten accumulation of pets' carcasses in piles.
A requiem for every bygone, fuzzy pal revisiting the yard
thinly disguised as a breeze or a chill,
or in the case of the more taciturn,
they want to come back as something louder,
a fart.
Bringing with them all their transmogrified little woodland friends
with whom, no longer bound by Darwinian etiquette,
they romp. A netherworld playground for roadkill.
The disembodied leading the disembowelled,
happy to be here, scratching, sniffing, humping,
dumping ghost turds on the lawn,
fearlessly.

It's no wonder so many bones surface,
surf the loam,
wheat heads advancing the cause like ants transporting a corpse.
Then the weeds pitch in the final mile,
hoisting femurs shoulder high.
They're dumped on the doorstep.

Or maybe it's just the dog
(the one who has survived thus far)
who brings these bones up to chew and then wanders away
taking parts unknown
to parts unknown.
Someday maybe, he'll chew on my bones.
Then, at last, I'll travel.

ambled, pig-snouted, hackle-backed mongrel, face all incisors and saliva, short distances from his straw grotto under the house. He chugged, puffed hostile gusts at the barnyard. Mornings, when he came out, he'd leave a moist, steamy coil between the wheelruts of the driveway. Strategically camouflaged. Premeditated hunkering in the crabgrass, ears up, Mephistophelean, ancient bowels straining, cuspid sneer, jowls mucific, drooling spider silk.

He'd head off toward the kill shack to feed on guts or nuts, sniffing, pounding on arthritic joints, temper strung like cable.

We'd go for Moe just to hear the old man tell us touch him and you'll pull back a stump.
We'd dare. How close can you go?

Moe pulled his ears back, teeth barbed. We wondered how his face didn't split down the middle.

We growled back, gargoyled, communicated our contempt, in his wiry little language, for his not letting us touch him, roll him puppyish, roughly, make him chase cattle, tousle, tackle him off toboggans or horseback, boy-handle him.

Instead we just fought him with sticks, like a dragon.

COMBINE

This morning the road is liquid,
tangible, thrushes
flurry among the shadows, this morning
to walk is to bathe, cool, canopied,
slowly, heat rises, buoys you
in this private Orinoco.
Martins perform morning aeronautics, fly-bys twisting the scrub,
morning knows how brown bats fold themselves
like itchy laundry under the eaves and that
raccoons, red foxes, barn cats thievishly retire,
to make way for the machinery of the day.

There is a daughterness about this time
and you are a son.

Day coughs diesel spits carburation binds hoses together with baler
twine trips to town lubrication greasy side-pork sandwich wedge pump
action shot vet shot bluestone holy hellfilth&foul fire&brimstone
cracked block spark motion fluid as transmission distribution catalytic
conversion quota mileage tonnage fetal manouevers offal sacs and
sacks of spillage

vagabondage

Night opens, star-chimed. All the molten world runs away.
Aurora hisses, strands raking each other.
You shiver off the day, peer curious into its insides,
ascend, rung by rung, augered into the process,
drop into the hopper, huddle, condense.
Allis Chalmers, the red of rust all that is left of sunset.
You are husked, the day that scratches like chaff blown away,
that secret skin left to lie, surface torn, waiting to be turned under.

Address the sky, wait for the grain to surround you,
sun fed, poured aloud from the dark machinery.
You are a son.

COOT

Legend and lore, look no further.
Here is the true trickster, esoteric bird,
resolute, pitch black canny, beaked not billed,
we can barely decide what to name you.
Slough pump, slough hen, mud hen, mud chicken, slough puppy.
Raven derived and rain driven, chug across the murk,
propelled by wave spanks,
directionless, mugwump hydraulics, rowing like a piston.
The ducks, the teal, the snipe are reeding along the shore;
you hammer your short-burst wake,
hauling headlong into palsy mist, reckless species, knowing well how
your station protects you.

And if some boy were to take a poke at you from the shore with a
twelve-gauge,
you would laugh the laugh of the web-heel damned, a great canard,
knowing that the youth, green to the hunt, would think he had bagged
his first mallard.
As the pellets penetrated, you would float, downy underside up, to the
centre of the slough, drag the boy into your death spiral,
laugh to teach him his first great lesson of the hunt —
the principles of retrieval.
Don't step beyond the bounds of your hip waders.
You will get no more than you aim for.

BLUE HERON

Out here at the stop sign, by the hull of Heron church, I am what
passes for traffic. Time, place, this creature, me — a cold grid
intersection. God's humour when He's too tired to be subtle.
A heron, ferrous blue, retracts its neck into a question mark
plumped on a feathery period, perched on standards that parade it like a
banner. Those skinny legs
                              reflected
the shadow self on the water like a net trolling for the truth in this.
It cranes its head up and away from itself, a pause in the introspection,
and retreats back into the bubble of its breath.
Legs like reeds, bill long and slender like a reed
              on a Birdland tenor sax set down on a wire stand.
Its namesake across the road is shut up,
aspenite over the windows,
siding cracked and weathered to a stubbly yellow.
The church buzzes with a congregation
of wasps circling their hung-to-dry home. Strands of foxtail brush
folk music out of the step rails, fingers plucking a testimonial.
The grass grows long in the marshy ditch.
The sky above is old. Wind hunches low, in eddies,
tired bits of cyclone, having blown everything out from their centre.
I would play the scene out, Fellini style. The great bird would spread
its wings, lift itself from the mire, soar out and back over the pasture
and upward
to circle, wings spanned and legs stretched   a cross
                              the last communicant
                    a banner over —
me in the centre of the crossroad, pinned in this junction. I would have
a lath crucifix nailed to the roof peak, rounding out the Trinity
of holy materialism.
But the spire blew down in 1978 and
              the heron seems content to peruse the muck and lengthen
the shadows. There is no point in scaring it off. So

24

I, like the departed brethren,
hop in the car, signal, turn left
and drive deeper
into what I expect to see

next.

Del T. and the Age of Jazz

Delmer Thiessen drops his keys
in the fretful snow, forages through the white, feels the fingertips
nipped alive like the cut from a string across the arc
of the playing field. He listens to the construction wrap-up backdrop,
the backbeat of beat-up truck cap lock snaps,
tossed tool box cacophony, cell phone touch tones,
honey, on my way home,
just a quick one at the Keystone.
He shakes the snow off his keys,
massages away that rhythm of the country night air. Like rubbing a
bone hurt. Leaves the pung-pong cattle drive two stroke diesel bass to
the hicks and kickers on the crew.
Del T. is headed for the jazz lounge at the south end of 13th Street,
where the music cross-circuits the night and everything seems to want
to fill everything else's gaps.

The call would go out when Del's parents would take a weekend
retreat or head to the city for Mennonite Central Committee meetings.
Amps into trunks, old Epiphone's wore new Dean Markley strings,
mickeys into coat pockets, girlfriends abandoned with throwaway lines
from the top 40   *me 'n the boys'll be playin'*
                                                all night.
Thundering marathons of arena rock anthems. Meaty handfuls of
three chord, Marshall stack growlers, extended drum solos
like boiler problems, bass riffs like intestinal gaffes. Swells and swells
of hit and miss power chord casualties blown out to the legions
of swooning poplar leaves hanging upside down from the rafters
above the cheap seats. Stars flicked lighters for encores.
The day gears down like a Jaco Pastorius bass line, high strung
tension timbered
popping   fibrillating at its apex bridging down
                                                down   tear drop
drowning
pulse loaded   and bloated feeling for the basement like a kid
who's found

the secret of the tuning key   pluck rattles off the bridge to
a flatulent tonal
zero.

In the days before he discovered John Lee Hooker, BB King, the delta
sound, John Hammond, Del T. listened over and over
to Randy Bachman imitating Lenny Breux, 9ths and diminished chords
sandwiched in a smear of industrial overdrive. It was one of the few
albums to escape the purge after Del's parents discovered the
handcrafted poster for the band's one nighter at the High School
Freshie Dance. The band was called Blackfinger.
His penance for 2 years was to play only acoustic 12 string for the
church folk choir until he finally convinced the elders that an electric
bass could fill in the bottom range. So Del T. cut his chops on the
bottom two strings of a five string Yamaha bass. The top three strings
waited, tempting and exotic. Forbidden.
Two strings   punk   pung   punk   pung
the passionate cadence of a windshield wiper.

Del's guitars resurfaced at the farm dispersal auction amid the
housewares and the muscled humps of machinery waiting for the
flatbeds. He watched them sell between the small Hammond organ
and the green floral print sectional. The Fender Mustang, the 12
string, the dreadnaught with the hole in the pick guard. He bought the
five string bass with the worn bottom strings, threw it in its case and
threw the case into the back of the truck. He stayed for lunch,
watched the albums sell in lots of 10, shuffled and dealt to the highest
bidder, right after the butcher knives.

The day ends, wash of smoke   small waves of table talk foam
single malt shuffle. Del's beachhead   his island of Pilsner and
Clamato and clatter
of glass washer tip-back   slow evaluation of the crash cymbal
and his ashtray. The guitar shanks the chords, sticks out,
the treble too hot, pick too thick like a thorn sticking

out of moss. The drumbrush snakes back
                          trips   recovers
                                      syncopated stumble,
choreographed pratfall
a no-news touch of the Mississippi blues.
It's the bassman that Del T. watches
            looking for that steal up the register
dreaming for himself that lunatic dexterity. The bassline scrambles
            up the rosewood, four fingers
stretching across four strings   winding and stretching like
                                      a moon crazed spider
attacking the crotch,
            spinning triads on the neck   tickling a formula and licking up
the last of night   lowering
                          on a fat thread   belly full and blue
                          blue blue blue not
                          even thinking 'bout
                                      plunkin' out
                                            a   polk
                                                  a.

Hey.
Now there's a conceptual breakthrough
blue on grey-blue over the prairie, where the sun spots some leverage
and cranks the cumulus for a quick meditation
on optics before jumping off the roof and landing in the lap
of the drearily departed sky.
Sun winks at the farmers giving them all the lowdown on what's up,
weeks of rain, crops festering in the fields.
Everybody's pissed off down here — if they thought they could crack
the sky with a rifle
they'd damn sure try
like the hunters from Kingston who pulled in last weekend to tramp
the swaths and squat
in the pits dug by the land owners, farmers sick of geese and wet
wheat and ducks
to the point they couldn't care less who shoots who or gets stuck in the
approaches as long as they don't have to haul their sorry asses out.
No anti-Eastern sentiment here.

The airspace between earth and sky fills with shot.
Hunters dream of birds falling
from the sky like ripe plums, speared on the stubble.
The geese narrow their Vs,
wagging their wings like pairs of long, upturned fingers.
If they felt any danger, they'd just climb a few more feet into the mist.
Clouds tumble into
their slipstream, cinch up tighter.
One hunter stretches up from the muck
figuring he's better off taking aim at the ground with his hat.

Healing Ground

I am what I am and I is where I are and what the hell do I care
about this land being removed by statute   twice removed spiritually
all the dirt I ate as a kid   on tractors   falling off horses
in the summerfallow
fistfights behind the toolshed   the devil-may-care-daring done
on this proving ground
the double dares that cramped me into breathless knots
the synapse snap that left me prostrate, grounded, lungs akimbo
after leaping off the stoneboat and hog-tying the dog
the salt and naphtha mustiness —
                                    hard to swallow

what's to miss out here   walking in the way of the dead
ghosts of horses charging the willows
the whiplash grin of the boy who rides just far enough in front to snap
me on my ass
with a gnarl of bush
the bones of animals stacked   ribs cantilevered
in the deadfall overgrowth
of a one-time basement
property filled with the sinkholes of good intentions
step around the dreams
pits   postholes   wire wiener sticks   cultivator shovels swaddled in
ragweed and nettles
metal rims   bones   more bones like outcroppings
magpies heyrocking sightlessly seamed into the rafters
of a mackerel sky

home to all this   what choices have I made not to be here
roots cut and dripping   like veins of a kill hung to bleed out
you try to heal where you have to

PIONEER

Peony blossom swells, ripens, a bright areola on a wash of white
sneezewort clusters
who live the summer as pearls. Pokes through the concatenation,
loosely spreads raw pink like a stain on lace work,
flashes its *je m'en fou* attitude,
chaos bristles on a woody stem, more benign than the rose.

The gardener comes to tend to this impudence.
She is slow, and orderly.
She beams to see that you have suckered your way along
to erupt here like an impatient memory.
To root it out would tear up the bed, and she is tired,
near the end of the day.

She runs her thumb and forefinger along the stem, thinking to pinch it
for a rose bowl.
The stem twists, sinks a willowy splinter into her thumb
before the prize surrenders. Surprised at this sudden wound
the crimson into the stem.
The petals absorb the colour with indifference.

She cups the blossom in her hand,
walks into the house to run water
over their wounds.

After the bloom has shrivelled, there is no grief. She begins to feel the
unwelcome blossom inside her skin
kinetic pioneer, playing
flutter and claim, flight and claim
through her landscape, roots too extensive to excise.
She does not grieve.

It is the last of love,
past want, care, burden, need or knowing,
a kiss in an exiled age of finally only being
that kills.

GOODBYE

If you mean to say goodbye,
it won't be on your terms —
grunting and sweating, agape with winter breath,
absorbed in fiddling or whipping horse flesh,
scheming the wares from your cronies
to trade them back again next week for promises of another day's work,
kicking over the salt licks until they are four cornered, pristine,
happily hardening your arteries into testy spines,
shrivelling your spleen into an appendix wart,
seeding this quarter of a quarter section with late summer rust.

If you mean to say goodbye,
it will be with me
in a house of your medical contemporaries
with white linen and order mocking you.
You will have a Bible as your concubine,
living in the backyard of your childhood independence
and hearing your schoolmates expire,
feeling the marrow-thin bones and cartilage conspiring to consolidate
into an amalgam of venous paste.
Staring at the seascapes your sisters mailed you.
Reading Rabbi Ben Ezra.

Seeing all and still
being afraid.

I wanted to hear your standard salutation, the snort and
    "well, what you don't see when you don't have a gun"
instead of the shaky drum roll rake-rap of your fingers on the bar
    top and a leathery cough. Your wife's hand is firm between the
blades of my back, marshalling me to an audience with an
    unwilling dignitary. Pushing me through the confessional
door. She comes back with tea. I only wish I knew the words to say
    how much I wish the beer were colder if I still drank
like I used to. If only there were a Canadiens game on the tube,
    I'd cheer against the Habs just to rattle your cage if only I were
sure your bones wouldn't break. I wish I still cared enough about
    the corporate culture of our profession to curse the new
administration, or that I had become administration.
    Just for tonight, you could coach, I'd play quarterback.
You'd engineer the plays, I'd call the audibles.

Smoke from your cigarette drifts along your shirt sleeve, rolls off
    the ash grey of your neck, your jaw, dissolves
into the murky web of the corkboard wall. Your silver hair is long,
    drawn back with your face. Your brush cut's gone AWOL,
like my words, your hairline retreating, derelict of duty. Your face
    is pitted, caulk grey, and wants, like the walls, to be
smoothed by absorbing the details of our lives. The rack
    on the wall is empty; the Remington is gone, the British 303
you inherited from your father after he died. His was the first
    of the father funerals. Though I didn't know what to say,
I stayed long enough for you to have seen me. I wish you had
    seen me. The rifles are gone and I wonder if you've already
given them to your boys.

Do you miss the hunts? You would take Jimmy and I
    slough hopping for canvasbacks or teal. You laughed about
the day Jimmy and I brought a small mallard down with a
    simultaneous shot and we argued over which of us
had hit the bird because it flopped around on the bank only

wounded and neither of us had the guts to take it by the head
and twist. We panicked as you rounded the bush
            until I raised my gun and blew its breast open. You had seen,
shook your head, mumbled something about great white hunters
            and then told us that at least I'd had the sense
not to abandon it to die slow.

My visit is limited to what your wife feels you are prepared to take:
            tonight thirty minutes. Few of those minutes have gone by.
Our talk is strained through the lumps in our throats. You twist the
            water in your glass; your medication makes no allowances
for whiskey, flick your cigarette to life again.
            We sit together, mostly silent, in your downstairs bar, sober
as judges. And wish we weren't.

THREE BROTHERS

There's a disturbing quality about the counterman at the old
Stationhouse cafe. Beyond a hiccup, an acceptable perturbation
in the norm.
He sells papers to the locals. Charges what he should.
Leaves a welt in the consciousness; presence ripples.
He excites talk.
When he smiles at the clientele,
teeth exotically parted in the middle,
hair black, features olive,
he generates subversion among
the denizens of coffee row.

Greek, ain't he?
From Yorkton, I hear.
   . . . used to run the cafe on the corner of Betts and Broadway.
   . . . Jes' lookit all the Greek stuff on the menu now . . .
         . . . Hear he's got family lookin' into buyin' the hotel . . .
   . . . Not the hotel, jes' the restaurant . . . they don't run hotels . . .
   . . . they jes' run the restaurants . . . How many of 'em ?
         . . . Wot? . . . Greeks?
No . . . in his family.
   . . . There's a Greek runnin' the Motor Inn cafe over in Wadena . . .
could be his brother . . .
   . . . Naw . . . brother to the one in Wadena runs the one downtown
   . . . in Wynyard.
   . . . well, they could still be brothers . . . ?
         . . . Yeah, they got pretty big families I gather . . .
Catholics, right?
   . . . Sure . . . you know, like Greek Orthodox.
Got kids? . . . None in school.
         . . . looks pretty young. Wot's his name?
   . . . Something . . . odakis . . .
That's the whole name?
   . . . No, jes' the ending.

. . . Yeah, us'd t' be every little town an' piss stop on the highway
had a Chinese cafe. Now everyone's gotta Greek.
  . . . Yeah, that's true . . . wonder what Ming thinks about all this . . . ?

Wickstrom, Extram, Schenstrom, Nordmarken, Nordhagen,
Kvemshagen, Templeton, James, Prouse, Kolchesky, Derenewsky,
Tychysny, Olcesnyk, Lullibo, Nakrayko.
Mothers and fathers. Each with a title, a claim.
No property liens, even through the '30s.
At least until wheat prices fell, and the kids overextended themselves.
Wedding dances at Rosebud Hall. Third generation,
fourth cousin marriages, air pungent with cabbage and kielbasa,
ripe with presentation and passage. Familiar.
Domestic as moonshine.

  . . . Wonder if he bought the place?
. . . Probly worked out a term lease . . . see if it was worth keepin' . . .
Nope. Heard he laid out the whole sum . . . one shot . . .
. . . Tom'd know . . . his daughter in law works at the bank.
. . . Aww, he wouldn't take a loan out locally . . . probly got his credit
    back in Yorkton . . .
Not wot I heard. Tippy says there was no financin' involved at all . . . jes
    plop with a cheque . . . Think he's good for it?
What makes you think he ain't . . . if he sold out somewhere else . . .
. . . besides those Greek families always stick together . . .
kinda a communal affair . . .
Mmmmm . . . kinda makes you wonder eh?

Two denim shortsleeves yank down the Drink Coca Cola
Stationhouse sign from its grainy perch, wrestle a whitegoldgreen
monolith into the hoist bucket. Noisily rivet in synch
with the low gear grind of grain trucks.
The yards long beacon opens to birch speckled sun
in defiance of land titles and local opinion.
    Three Brothers Licensed Dining

. . . Three Brothers . . . hmph . . . told you so.

Nice sign . . . musta been from that outfit outta Melfort . . .

. . . Naw . . . truck's got Manitoba plates . . . probly Swan River . . . where *Jimmy C. got his sign for the auto body.*

. . . C'mon, let's go in . . . Stan's turn to buy coffee.

The hell it is . . . Who paid yesterday?

. . . Licensed Dining . . . mmmmmm . . . what time does he *open up the lounge?*

Welcome home

Reflections on a Track Record

Moonlight overtakes station lamp
lights lock on a rail
steel ghost slices open the belly of the prairie
at obtuse angles
air
quicksilver cool
bathes itself in a hybrid scent
lilac, clover,
creosote wrung from the ties
by worlds away heat
sky repositions itself
pulses to a cricket cadre
silver seams stitch together the worlds of
men
jiggers and tie jacks
beer parlour
hydraulics
and of
boys
searching idly for detonator caps
daring each other not to lose fingers
daring each other who would be the first
to touch the farm girls who slept in houses
along the rails

BACON

that lollipop
        salt-lick crisp
    in the folds crackle
        of fresh currency
    maple style or
        hick
                or y
                    or pepper slab
                pre-fab
local smoke
            house or
            mass marketed tossed on
a sesame seed bun
with special
    sauce McBacon or
    maybe McSwine for
me who has eaten your
                farrow nine
            fat-char haze that
                crows good
                    morning sweet nitrate
            the no shirt laziness of frying bacon
        Sunday before church
            flavour that ol'
                factory time religion
    is good enough for me
                torso blossoming into
                thermal measles
                    grease pop accupoints that needle
you awake
the cook is lazy but
the meat jumps with the kinetics of the
stock exchange
                        that killing
floor

here   are   the tools
      rock&switch
      cone&drum
            either bang away or
      scrub the mission

confluence of clicks whirrs pops
    belches and farts
        languid
                motions flashes curves blinks and
clangs clang clang went the bells

    language

someone creates the invisible one
                  o h o
                  one
                        stream
some one else the universe with five hundred channels
and four tacks

assertive: I   think I
              can   I think
    I   con

interrogative?: How am I doin' so far
                    darlin'

imperative>: b u y t h i s

exclamatory: !buy this! (insert   hyper
                            cat y lec
tic telemarketing rant
                here)!

the little first words

                    mom
           out of the baby's mouth piggy back a
subtext:

                         you are here for
                                        ever
                                        and ever I am
                                               safe

a bold   in your
      faced   type — Chicago gangster font
           lie

The ambulance bubbles flash get the hell out of the way
to the railway crossing lights pumping back off — everything
working a quarterflash off synch with everything else
immovable object rumbles across the highway slowing
for the siding switch ahead the irresistible force
Colville's horse heading for clover
the long way
                    around the conical banshee wailing off spirits
                                        wailing of lost babies
wailing the switchman awake&all these little capillaries
hemorrhaging red into the night
                                        no discussion of right
           of way
The language is perfectly clear   all we have
here is a failure to capitulate

home

subtext: stable

       where the heart is

wanna bop the drum better dream about the timing
   work on the rhythm say to hell with the rhyming
the this
       this
and the that that that of
the underground sprinkler nozzle popping up a pressure
       driven mole spitting against the siding&reminding
that during your two week vacation
that the sky opened two or three times daily hailing or raining
that your credit union rain gauge overflowed its banks
  & abandoned ship
that was six days ago
that this sinkhole remnant of
that long gone septic system opened into a makeshift storm drain
that caused the seam in the foundation to purse into
this vision of the house & its hose hydraulics all meandering down
this slope toward Wolverine creek with all the basement boxes full of
these precious tomes
        boxes   boxes of poems
    the tracts of my tears all
this sewage draining downstream toward the cattle who may not even
    choose to ruminate on
this

play

subtext: blow that horn Gabriel
                    to beat the band
        subtext: (double-indemnity) god looks after fools and drunks
sub

here they come with the hey
just like i told you so bubble gum flash and
their caterwauling sonic levity
the Saturday night nine cats on a fence dance
you pray to god it degenerates into a doppler whine on
the way by but
nope
you're implicit in the audience my honky tonkin
friend
pull over
            momma's boy
    get set
to tow the line walk the line
the thin blue line between you and:
            yourself
we're not in Can
                    a der any more,
Dor o
            thy no no   this
is tourism Texas style where your mind punctuates the
Mirandizing with snatches of Johnny Cash tunes,
                    boots, batons, bail judgements
                        frames from Turkish prison flicks
if you wanna dance
                    you gotta play   to beat
the band

drum

subtext: the fun is in playing by ear

coda
blue true blue where the heart is

running that er

ra   ta tat

tic stop[

time] syncopated the audio
feed of this schizoid movement peeled off and   re
corded crescendo pizzacatto arrhythmia
the score will soon be on paper
the cone fed string&horn section rests
the clang clang clang of the trolley

rests

that metronome sound of a key turning
above is the mechanism of the flashers ticking
just above the near ghost
of someone's mom the clock
tocking taking stock itty bitty
little pulse of circuitry chit
chat ears
filled with the L.A.N.

gauge of body parts

stinging
chitty chitty

bang
bang

A Pair of Boots

There's a pair of boots sticking up out of the CNR ditch, their chrome toeplates pointing to magnetic north. They're claiming the right of way, suspended apparently by a hardy strain of thistle. I wonder why these boots are still here, their beaks aimed skyward. Some forthright soul like myself could try to return them to their rightful/leftful feet. Or why haven't they been carried off by the likes of Marcel Gaudré, who surely must have made his morning pass down this stretch of road allowance, trolling for empties to buy more Strawberry Angel?

And if by some chance the boots are attached to a wearer, languishing downward, so much the better. I assume the boots are broken in. The removal will be a quick procedure; I'll push the heel to the toe, wrestle with give and take, and in no time I'm on my way. And if the feet come off with the boots, better yet; I'll have replacements for my tired dogs. Or else now I'll use all four, too much is made of being bipedal. Now, if the knees come with them, then excellent; I've been meaning to replace those whiny hinges on the back gate; these will only crackle arthritically in cold weather. If I drag off the buttocks, I'll have a splendid pelvic planter or a simulation porcelain bird bath. And if the torso follows, more power to me. A ribcage hat rack would cause such a sensation, more evocative than the twelve point jackelope head we use at the Shell coffee bar on 83. Or if I'm really lucky, I'll get the arms too . . . sweet heavenly jackpot: the slung over the bathroom door back-scratcher/towel holder/point the index fingers together toilet roll dispenser. Everyone will want one.

But not the head . . . oh no . . . that would not do. Because then you'd be dragging home a corpse, or worse yet the town drunk . . . no one in the world would be caught dead with Marcel Gaudré at their house, especially when you'd discover that he'd swiped the boots from the dry goods store and you would be obliged to return them without a receipt. In our town, in that great spirit of poetry, we've agreed to communally defy convention, and hold firm to our conviction that the sum of the whole is definitely less than its parts.

How Deer Breathe in Three Dimensions

On the cusp of morning,
some downdraft trickle
sparks the fireplace back to life.

Fire makes no noise
        beyond a knot-pop staccato.

Sparks court fuel.
Fire digs through the ashen grave of itself
and wishes for groves.
It catches bark.
Logs collapse.
A final reconfiguration of flame
catches an updraft —

a principal cue.

In silence she steals.
She works her cloven way
over the snow-covered railroad bed,
flanks the radius of light, a ponderous intersection,
and crosses thoughtless as a corpse into
an urban existence.
Hoof clanks
        a culvert.

Hint of crime here —
                of intent.
Sinister stroll through a pale land where
nighthawks are regaled with the snap of locks.

She peels back a layer of trunk
cold to the touch
if a touch has nerves.
Bares white wood,
tears skin silver as rime.

She plucks off the last of the apples,
fawn speckled with frost,
forsaken,
ice-eyed.

Slowly she comes. Leans to the light, feigning timid.
Response beyond instinct, her steps are callous, premeditated,
invasive.
She gazes through the window pane, where she postures to breathe.
If she can hear the death sizzle
of the fire,
she doesn't respond.
Fire makes no noise.
Where she vents her breath, steam forms.
Not flat, milky disks, that kids revel in,
but perfect globes, studied in symmetry.
Glacial pustules adhered to glass. Two perfect eyes.

The fire sinks.

She does hear the sun rise.

Early Evening Aerial

The late afternoon fly-over confirms
that this village
exists a single community
with committees of lesser constituents
squarely in the middle of nowhere
unconnected
no rail line (not near Elbow, Eyebrow, Navel)
no elevator (white wooden phallic husk: true residency)
no highway (no way to validate your presence in the body politic,
the scorched earth policy)

only a gravelly tributary occasionally pumps a
vehicle's dust into your system
a peopled little carcinoma
ashamed not to be a product of economics
existing, independent of a service hub philosophy
a cultural construct, geared to a
white clapboard gyrocentre (*Episcopal, I think*
having quite intentionally
I think how, God floated
settled into the nowhereness of where this is
I think how, God, somebody thought you up)

in the southwest corner, the motor hotel and the implement dealership
form a dendrite
seems to want to hook up to a creek
cleanse itself in the distant Red
civil disobedience over civic planning

the corporate limits are
a watery membrane (wired thin enough to let the chickens out and
let the foxes in)
they don't smell the parts
they see this place as a whole
a blight and only when it is lit
in the darkness

DARK HAMLET

phantom of pressboard cola sign
kinks, shards
spike rough rock bed
peeks through the demographic and lets you know that
something built once
was there
tiger lilies and crocuses testify
play border symbols
pending legal definition
gopher holes orbit post-hole depressions
poles having been surreptitiously sucked by machines
wrenching like kids pinching white milk out of stems
poles laid trackside
carried off on flatcars then rails plucked up
carried off by trucks
ties
carried off by landscapers to dam a garden
stacked and tumbling where phlox runs down like water
deer and skunks and wolf willow run off with the road
moss pushes up platform knotholes
pushes at the stars
blue as insulator glass
Cassiopeia covers herself in a
silk shroud of cloud
lays on thick garments
the way she did the night the heavens
opened Biblically
breathed rivers into road allowances
stole back the fire
spanked clapboard recalcitrants
breathed barometric
tore up wheat stems and missiled the heads
felled crops under an icy flail

cold thresher spun into cone

blows out ghosts
breathes in
leaves you to ponder a new geometry
quiet in timber time
listen to the madrigal of owls invite new citizens

BRIDGE AT ST. LOUIS

Dense waves of morning slope onto the foot of the bridge at St. Louis.
Camera lens, in spite of refined optics, registers only gradients of light,
greyscale. Defines the world in negative, inverse logic controlled.
But I can't wait for the day to improve.

In the instant the shutter opens, a shadow shows in the milky
cloud/sky/river merge dark, the colour of bushline
vanishes in the view field, with shutter speed. Some watery dune,
or a shorebird perhaps, shaped like a body. Mist lodges in hair.
Revise angle, adjust exposure. A second form approaches upstream,
clearly revealed in the synapse quarter second snap,
featureless, free-form shadow, a body all the same, flowing rigid,
centre cast, immutable
in that instant like the river in full freeze. Gone.
Hawk traverses the treeline, banks low, alerted to presence.
Senses altered.

The morning shudders. I have no equipment for this
sensual terrorism. Brown wrinkle of high bush cranberries,
faded blush of rose hips resolve into the alloy
of leaves. A triumvirate of hawks circles above the village, spirited up,
river scavenges the bank.
Eye as trickster, this dull mechanism ponders thin creepers and these
loamy shadow-corpses
the dispossessed surfacing hatch-veined like mossy weeds cracking
the asphalt on the St. Louis Bridge

Riel	disturbing the rushes
Dumont	caught in back flows, the Saskatchewan
Helen Betty Osborne	oxbows
J. J. Harper	meandering the Qu'Appelle
Charlotte Ayowapace	the Assiniboine
children of Davis Inlet	the Red
channeling, drifting	

toward gulf or bay, harbingers.
Bird strafes the water, hawk or eagle, obscured in mist, ascends
sifts into cloud,
visible through this camera, by this little village that knows the river.

51

CONTROLLED BURN

1

Haze cross-cuts the highway, merges into a curve
churns in the car's slipstream
everything is aware of dirt burn
deer stir in the bush, immured
beyond the fire line.
Small, round faces,
children moonlit through windshield, side windows
dream
palls of smoke
drift just between euphoria and earth
smoke low cast, charged with amber
stubble fire embers dance to their flashpoint
metre drawn constellations sink
into line thin indigo, cultivated firebreak.
Night slides by in quarter sections.

2

Between the headshaft and a mountain of effluent
a kid sweats his first day working the mill
of the potash mine
straps wooden clogs on to his leather soles
so he won't feel the burn, breathes slowly
his last cool. Steps into a product drier
which would fit ten men, but only two enter
in rotation
sweat drops, sizzles on the cones
kid bashes the potash cake out of the vents
swings through the hot leather haze, boot rivets heat,
panting
tools, hammer and punch, pulse through gloves
world degreed in minutes of cool.

3

At the glassworks, heat is orange, ripe
punty descends into glory hole, the medium is forged
reforged, resurfaces
radiates centrifugal form, Promethean
raw in its preconception
falls under the weight of tools, commits itself to shape
flexes in its birth dance, refines into
carbon cool, lines resolute and solid
its human counterpart still malleable in the remnants of heat

4

Double talk at the table:
impenetrable terrain, hostile environment, negative optioning, napalm,
terra incognita, airborne reconnaissance, collateral damage,
impracticality of land approach, concentrated engagement,
concentric purges, purviews and venues, hot avenues, sky hawks
and tomahawks, paths of no resistance — language of the highflown
and fireborn

5

Distant atmosphere, the sun,
rubs a corona around the earth, solders it to space
jets slow burn stabilize, rotate, re-orient, balance this vessel
in a lunar sling,
cold phoenix has risen high above its fire, still as the tropics below.
From here, infrared registers only
                    industry
                                        Hamburg, Dusseldorf, Brazilian forest
                    wattage
                                        Tokyo, London, New York
                    thermal inversion
                    of souls knotted
                    too closely
                                        Mexico City, Lagos
no measurement of stubble fires, prairie,
politics, or God.

53

6

A hundred years ago, prairie fires scourged the grasslands, burned
out tracts of poplar, willow.
Redistributed herds of deer, recharted feeding lands for waterfowl.
Fire, unchecked, reclaimed and rezoned
consumed bracken,
species retreated
surface growth stripped, re-invented in layers
soil slipped into new skin.

On the shore of Little Quill Lake, a willow clump twists itself into a
stranglehold
grows barky from the inside out, suffocates on itself.
It has seen the rise and ebb of the lake for a hundred years
dies in an age that is unnatural.

Children in the car sleep on.
Smoke from a dozen stubble fires has followed,
the highway dots blip by
tires descant above the internal combustion song.

KID WITH THE SWASTIKA

kid with the swastika on his arm
enjoys talking about
how the iconography came to be
one session at a time
a house of worship that grows by
porches and lean-tos
he says no matter what you've heard before
a good tattoo artist will never
hurt you the clockwise spines
are shaded toward the outer edges
giving relief the crucifix
emerges with the staves
extended beyond the kinks of
the swastika
those extensions left without dark rumbles
of ink his arm inside those shafts white the hair
on the arm thin almost albino
he shows me the blue filaments that intersect
the cross to form the Star
of David and how the Baha'i nine-sided
star plays off the radius of all the
interior trappings
shows me the entry points signifying
nine world religions i fear
to ask him which of the tattoos came
first
which last in that mosaic
radiating around a hairless white scallop in the centre
the scar
from a cigarette burn

THEFT IN THE PORCUPINE HILLS

Gravity grows heavy at the prospect of idly prairie loping
another open mile, ogles the landscape for some vague sign of
pre-Cambrian escape. Sees an outcropping of schist, curls in on
himself, rolls and rumbles, goes underground. Reverses the flow,
bleeds into the pores of a new domain. Lays his head on mantle,
feels roots tickle, kicks feet, comforted in ceiling, and propels the
horizon, a geomorphic restoration.

Hills rise, and rise. Gravity's other, moon, will not relinquish density,
resists with her only tool, tide on this plain defined as flora. Coniferous
weight pushes, the hills howl nightly, aria of entreaty for fronds to
uncurl double-time, for spinal reinforcement of moss, for pine needles
to tangle upper air aviaries, for ferns to grow allegro, bows striking cellu-
lose cello lows. Porcupines curl into balls.
Hills curl into balls.
Moose weight bound to resistance.

An instrumental gardener steals in the night, obscene, raw
mathematics in a musical equation.
Pokes a spade into septum,
cuts a figure, circle,
a semi-circle,
a piece of pi
rips the prize,
splay leafed trophy.
Moon ellipse casts surgical
into the sear, untimely rest in the boreal orchestration. A gap gravity
hadn't prepared for.

How to restore balance. How to reward this act.
Pot of twisted rhizomes dies in brown and curling grip
of ego.
Parched single note, poisoned with display.

Miles away, moon and gravity peer at each other through a cyclamen
scar, argue
over the principle of ownership.

Daughter's Gift to Open the Morning

You crouch in the seat of the car,
tired, cold.
I've made you rise, in my mind by agreement,
to rise
into the foothills,
to hoist you above the prairie, prescribing for you this epiphany
because I can.
All I wanted to give you, a gift for you to see the world climb
out of itself, rock face aspiring to sky above the straws of pine
that merge upward
into shag.
A gift of relief from your plain of existence
I wanted to see you make something of this new axis
from which suddenly elk,
or bears, or goats might tumble and spill
onto the roadside, and your voice
in its narrow moments might startle you from behind.
How will you deal with this sideways mysticism?
Jump to be perched on its shoulders?
Will you kneel, stoically,
sifting through the shale for agates?
Lean against a wall or lie against the roadside,
ear pressed to the cold, listening for seismic secrets,
rumours of further upheaval? Tune out the roadside whine,
the pressure gradient hum, hoping to hear something more holy than
grass or sky?

But Calgary is crowning white in the grey outside the car park, and
the skyline wanes as the pallor sifts in. Nevertheless, soon,
we will rise, launch into heightened awareness;
because I can,
I impose on you the grandeur of this grey green spillway,
stars, satellites,
grain elevators

pretenders to this elevation. The morning endures.
Snow line descends and squats in clouds,
nests in the crook of the Bow like a seagull
fat with plumage, full from plunder. Four lanes narrow
to two wheel ruts. The backdrop of the day vanishes sideways
in Etch-A-Sketch silver. I preach the vagueness of something
other than ourselves out there
beyond the veil.
Through the morning, we rise.

My gift has eluded you today;
you drift in and out of sleeping
inventing white tales to tell your friends when you return
home, from this storm that blows through the cusp of summer.
We turn,
descend to the safety of the city,
its trails bounded by useless grass.
I think you are as sad as I am
because I can only
imagine that you've lost your impression of the exotic,
its only appeal being familiarity. You've seen
what you've seen on any January day
on the prairie.
                    I drive,
blindly blizzard minded; you sleep
through the storm,
rapid eye moving horizontally so that I'd never guess
that you are dreaming of mountains.

PROCESS

Blizzard collapses.
Contrary to the physics of this moonless night, snow glows,
tapped into its own source,
plows into darkness, then reconnoitres,
    regroups in updrafts against houses
       and drifts,
darkness dampens in cold reduction,
  silver skin purges the earth
     of itself. Night shouts the senses alive,
air dry static heave, white
skyline ablation, wrinkles and vales
of landscape adopt their new uniform,
twitch grass tangles, erases.
     Fractals touch frozen skin; each refuses the union,
wind breathes
chaos, gravity intervenes, works a slow restoration,
kinetic cells
settle into equilibrium,
sky.

Birds sense the order, do not shriek in terror.
They huddle into the base of juniper, inflate themselves,
practised diagrams of feathers. Wait.
Some totter on branches, feign sleep,
instruments at rest, they listen to the wind's score while
the storm works its revision

RETREAT

Day recedes; evening camps,
squats in the seat of western hills,
divides its time between
quenching itself, pink/hot and furious,
into the Columbia, the Kootenay, the Fraser, and
casting its last channels vainly toward this premature snow shower,
working itself under the cloud shelf and
above the slant of trees. The snow crosses
in flurries, gangles in ghost troughs,
centres, and drops,
clings to the swaths in ready-made drifts,
moulds, all muscle, into ill-timed tension,
a father waiting for the birth of a child.

Snow, in this month, speaks to the users of the land, chides them
white noise wisdom rattles their panes,
says, "Squatters. Pull yourselves up; witness the ripening.
You sow, you sow, you reap sometimes and so on
but you never know —"
and families adhere to the windows, kids from the TVs,
husbands and wives from their beds, suddenly astonished not to see
their skin reflected.
Yard lights and street lights wink in morse code gusts.
Tabula rasa.
A cold climatic efficiency that a flood could only admire.

Snow fades just short of Drumheller
and the Horseshoe Canyon,
as though the storm knew that, on this day,
here was more geomorphology than it cared to handle.

CACTUS TALK

Verbal pickle, sticking vertically
                                out of the soil
peeking over the terra cotta, hide bursting with barbed tips of gossip
broadcasting expletives with an effective radiated power
                                of 25,000 pic-O-hurts
twenty-four hours a day
                         in a foreign language
antennae crackling with violent static —
        the sun's rays in a child's drawing, spearing passer-by looks
hooking and landing attention. Wise
like a grandparent's whiskery warning about the evils
        of self-abuse.

The need for touch is pathological.
                can't believe in isolation
                can't trust the nerve endings
                can cactus innards really sustain someone
                        dying of thirst?
Kids want to drum on the sides, test for acoustics,
                    even wind skirts around, looking for points of entry.
Cactus talk is the sound of alchemy at work, the prairie balled up
        on an August dog day,
house wrecking silence, noise that even water
                        can't abide.

CENTREPIECE

The wedding cake sits by a podium at the centre of the room.
Horseshoes fashioned into candle holders and
four-inch clay pots
       each with a cactus
anchor every table.
The bridesmaids in their Santa Fe neon
                   neo-Navajo print dresses
                                     spin
fabric twirling around their Tony Lamas the way
the women are orbited by the men in dark
tuxedo jackets over dark
jeans
silver belt buckles with agate centres
a green pining for a lick at the fireplace.
The kids are scattered through the large room
parcelled into groups in the
coarse beamed twilight.
The city kids flash faces into throw-away instamatic lenses;
the older kids congregate around the sound system
pleading with the DJ to pre-empt Patsy Cline
for the Macarena
while their parents dance away the last of
"Crazy". The prairie kids stare out
the west window toward the distant
craggy white caps pulling back from the white breath of the glass
dreaming of what's wild
up there

The uncles trowel the last of the cheesecake into themselves
marvel at the money still to be made out west, inspired by the
roughhewn rustic opulence
thinking now about seconds, hungry like a pack of voyeurs who've
just discovered a window-wide keyhole
                            oil
               everything out here runs on
      oil

The aunts have discovered the fruit flan and the champagne
and the throw-away instamatics. They've peeled the cardboard
covering from the cameras and, unencumbered by instructions,
ponder the mysteries of the on-board flash
chatter and fumble like monkeys with matches
soon no one's retinas will be safe.
The cacti squat in
their clay pots trimmed
in southwestern motif with fabric from
the bridesmaid dresses.
Our hands have been skirting the plants all night
tongues flirting with barbs as we
passed the sugar, the cream, the salt, please pepper, look the bride
and groom are
here it's starting to snow and it's only September my what an unusual
choice for a
centrepiece

These families come together too seldom for weddings
to love, honour, cherish
too often
for funerals

I'll have long forgotten the shape
colour texture
flavour of the wedding cake by the time my cactus dies. Perhaps it will
outlive me.
Once in a while, I'll set it in the centre of the table,
an occasional reminder that no one
nothing in this life
not even what lives on wind
passes the branches
lightly.